PIANO · VOCAL · GUITAR

Owl City
All Things Bright and Beautiful

CONTENTS

ISBN 978-1-4584-1382-6

HAL·LEONARD®
CORPORATION
7777 W. BLUEMOUND RD. P.O. BOX 13819 MILWAUKEE, WI 53213

Visit Hal Leonard Online at
www.halleonard.com

THE REAL WORLD

Words and Music by
ADAM YOUNG

*Recorded a half step higher.

DEER IN THE HEADLIGHTS

Words and Music by
ADAM YOUNG

Met a girl in the park - ing lot, and all I did was say, __
Met a girl with a grace - ful charm; but when Beau - ty met the Beast, __

__ "Hel - lo." Her pep - per spray made it rath - er __ hard __
__ he froze. __ Got the sense I was not her __ type __ by the black __

for me to walk her home. But I guess __ that's the way it goes.
__ eye and blood - y nose. But I guess __ that's the way it goes.

Tell me a - gain, __ was it love __ at first sight __ when

ANGELS

Words and Music by
ADAM YOUNG

DREAMS DON'T TURN TO DUST

Words and Music by
ADAM YOUNG

HONEY AND THE BEE

Words and Music by
ADAM YOUNG

KAMIKAZE

Words and Music by
ADAM YOUNG

The prin-cess in her flow-er___ bed___ pulled the jun - gle un-der-

ground, where cher-ry bombs___ stain the black-birds___ red___ and

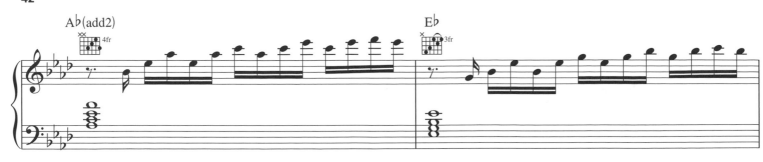

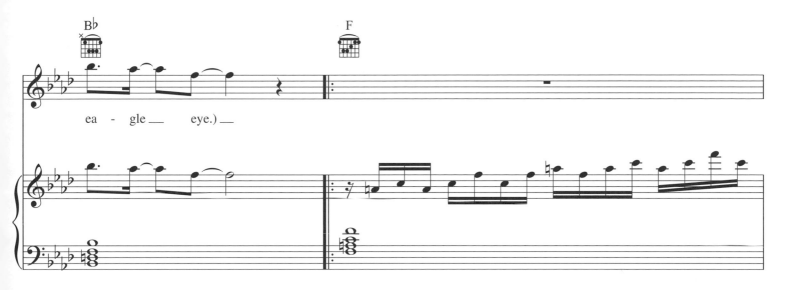

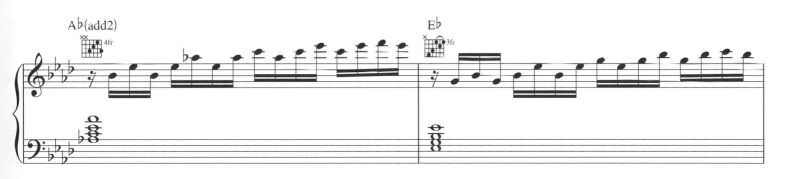

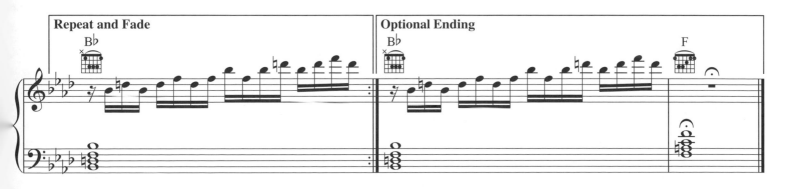

JANUARY 28, 1986

Words by RONALD REAGAN
from his speech following the Challenger disaster
delivered on January 28, 1986
Music by ADAM YOUNG

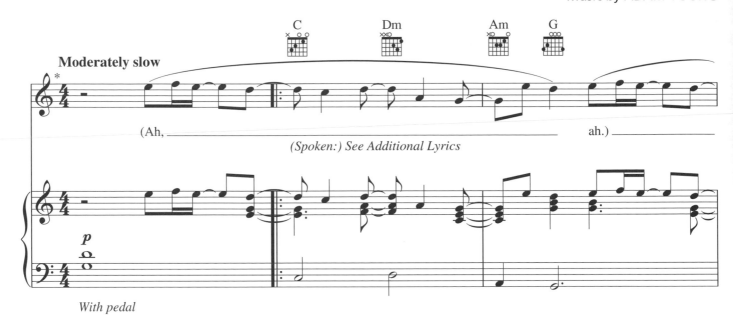

* *Recorded a half step higher.*

Segue to "Galaxies"

Additional Lyrics

(Spoken:) Ladies and gentlemen, today is a day for mourning and remembering. They had a hunger to explore the universe and discover its truths... And they had that special grace, that special spirit that says, "Give me a challenge, and I'll meet it with joy." The crew of the space shuttle Challenger honored us for the manner in which they lived their lives. We will never forget them as they prepared for their journey and waved goodbye, and... slipped the surly bonds of earth... to touch the face of God.

GALAXIES

Words and Music by
ADAM YOUNG

Moderate dance tempo

* Recorded a half step higher.

Dear God, I was ter-ri-bly lost when the gal-ax-ies crossed and the sun went dark. ___

But dear God, you're the on-ly North Star I would fol-low this far. ___

Instrumental solo

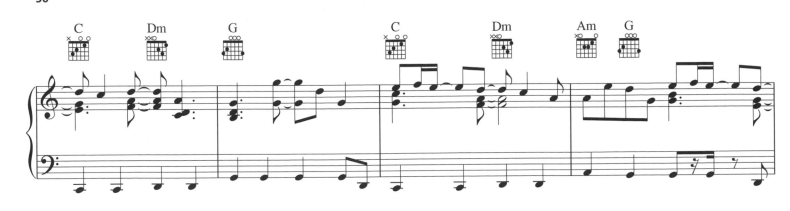

HOSPITAL FLOWERS

Words and Music by
ADAM YOUNG

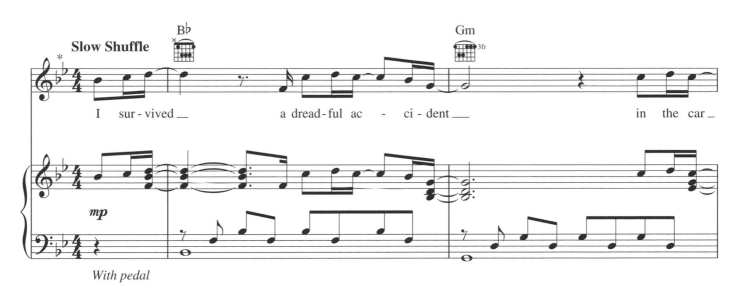

I sur-vived __ a dread-ful ac - ci-dent __ in the car __

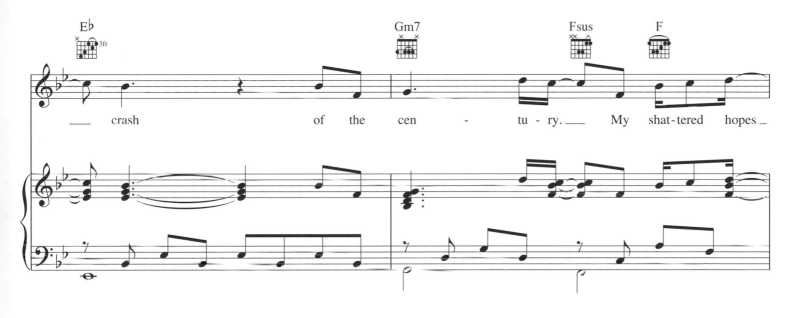

__ crash of the cen - tu-ry. __ My shat-tered hopes __

__ col-lapsed on cold ce - ment, __ but in the back of the

Recorded a half step higher.

ALLIGATOR SKY

Words and Music by ADAM YOUNG
and SHAWN CHRYSTOPHER

Additional Lyrics

Rap 1: Uh uh, that's not a plane, that's me! I'm sittin' where I'm s'pposed to.
Floatin' on a cloud, can't nobody come close to.
The concrete and the sky switch places,
So now my ceiling is painted with cosmic spaces.

Firecracker to the moon, keep your eyes shut!
Blastin' off like a rocket from the ground up.
Ha, I used to catch a cab on the Monday,
Now my taxi's sellin' lights on the runway... Fly.

Condo on the Milky Way;
A house on the cloud and God's my landlord.
And for my rent, all I pay is my drive;
I've got that. So if you need me you can find me in the alligator sky.

Rap 2: Aw, now I'mma dance like I never danced,
Sing like I never sing, dream like I never dreamed,
Oh, or tried to, 'cause we've been lied to,
That the sun is somethin' that we can't fly to.

Well, I sit on my star; I see street lights.
Look up, ah, you'll miss me if you blink twice!
Heh heh, imagination is high,
And if you got it, you can meet me when you see me in the alligator sky.

THE YACHT CLUB

Words and Music by
ADAM YOUNG

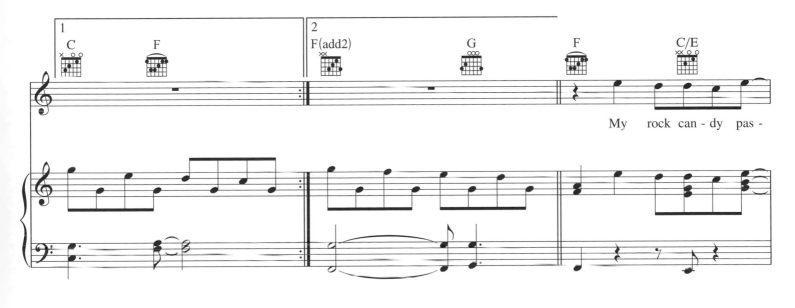

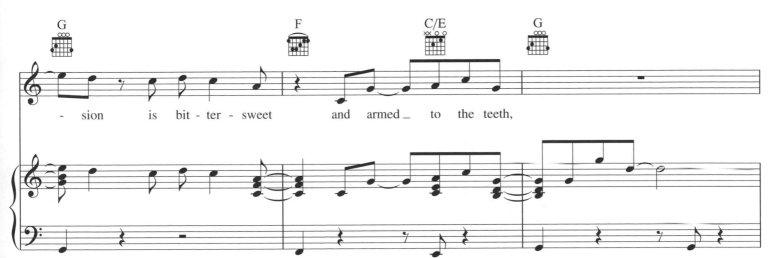

* Recorded a half step higher.

PLANT LIFE

Words and Music by ADAM YOUNG
and MATTHEW THEISSEN

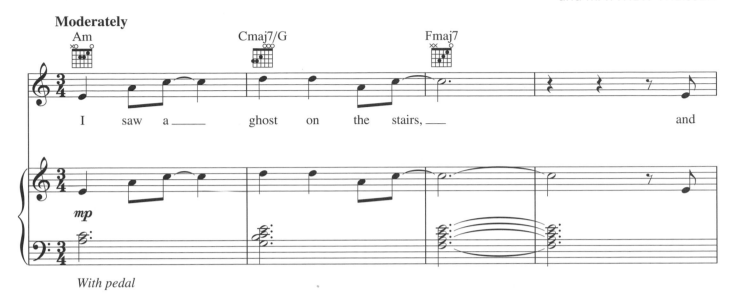

I saw a ____ ghost on the stairs, ____ and

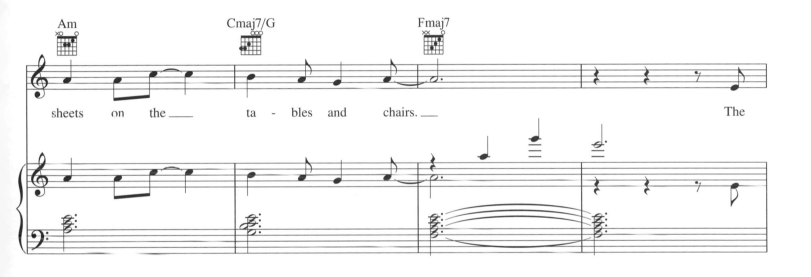

sheets on the ____ ta - bles and chairs. ____ The

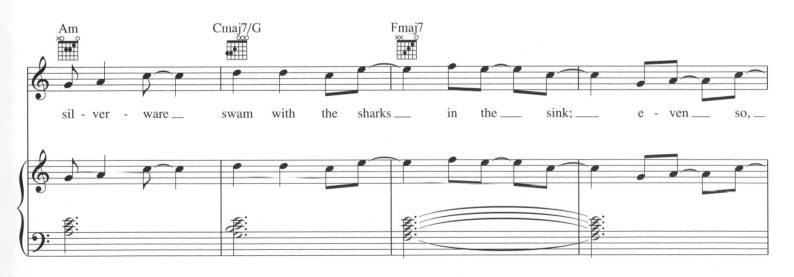

sil - ver - ware ____ swam with the sharks ____ in the ____ sink; ____ e - ven ____ so,

What Is My Job?

Every single person in our field needs an up-to-date job description. Period. This is one of the easiest things to overlook. In most cases, no one is going to do this for you. It is totally up to you.

Most of us go along year after year assuming that because everything is going well, it will continue to do so. We may begin our jobs with a current description that seems logical and appropriate.Over the years, things change. Duties are added. A few might be subtracted. More duties are added. We are filling in whatever gaps there are. No one really knows all of the various things we do in our job. They certainly won't know unless we document it! (Don't you just hate it when people assume that being a choral director is a "cushy" job or even worse, "I wonder what they do all week?")

Then something comes up, and someone usually new to the group, and asks, "Why isn't he/she doing such and such?" Or sometimes it may be "Why is he/she doing such and such?"

In many cases, the person or persons who hired us are no longer in the picture. To say, "Well, this was a verbal agreement when I took the job," will not suffice. It also won't work to say, "This is the way I have always done it." You need to have an updated job description for your protection, if for no other reason.

My suggestion is that you put at least one very important item on your yearly "To Do" list: **Update Job Description**.

Completing the task includes getting the appropriate people in positions of authority to sign off on it. This should be something you request every single year. The new job description will be attached to your annual evaluation and placed in your personnel file, for your protection, as well as that of your employer.

It should also include the goals that you have set for the next year on the job. The simple act of writing down everything you do will enlighten and even surprise you and definitely anyone else with whom you share it.

Life Highlights

The turning points may have been positive or negative. But the most important thing about each of them is that they taught you life lessons and eventually helped form the person you are today. This can be taken from a purely personal standpoint, or from the standpoint of your musical life. Sometimes, they are inextricable.

There are so many incredible outcomes from this exercise: not only for you, but for those around you – friends, family, coworkers, students. They will all benefit from you taking the time to do this. I can't encourage you enough to do this – for yourself, if for no one else.

Here is a sample.

Life Highlights

Age	Year	Event	People Involved	Environment	Feelings
0					
1					
2					
3					
4	1955	Romper Room	Mother	TV Studio	Failure
5	1956	Voice Lessons	Mother	Home	Curiosity
6	1957	Kindergarten	Teacher	School	Fun!
7	1958	Move	Family/Friends	New Town	Insecure
8	1959	Move	Teacher/Friends	New School	Comfortable
9	1960	Art	Teacher/Family	Home	Hurt
10	1961	Talent Show	Friends/Family	Public Performance	Accomplishment
11	1962	Football	Bobby/Scott	Team	Really BAD!
12	1963	Playing Bass	Teacher	Orchestra	New Musical
13	1964	...pping	Jewish	Neiman M...	Paridigm
14	1965	...der			
15	1...				